Stars in the Sky

CeCe Wilson

Rosen REAL READERS

Rosen Classroom™
New York

I see stars in the sky.

Stars are in outer space.

They are billions of miles away.

Stars are hot balls of gas.
There are millions of stars
in the sky.

The sun is a star.

It is the closest star to Earth.

The sun is very hot.
It is about
10,000 degrees Fahrenheit.

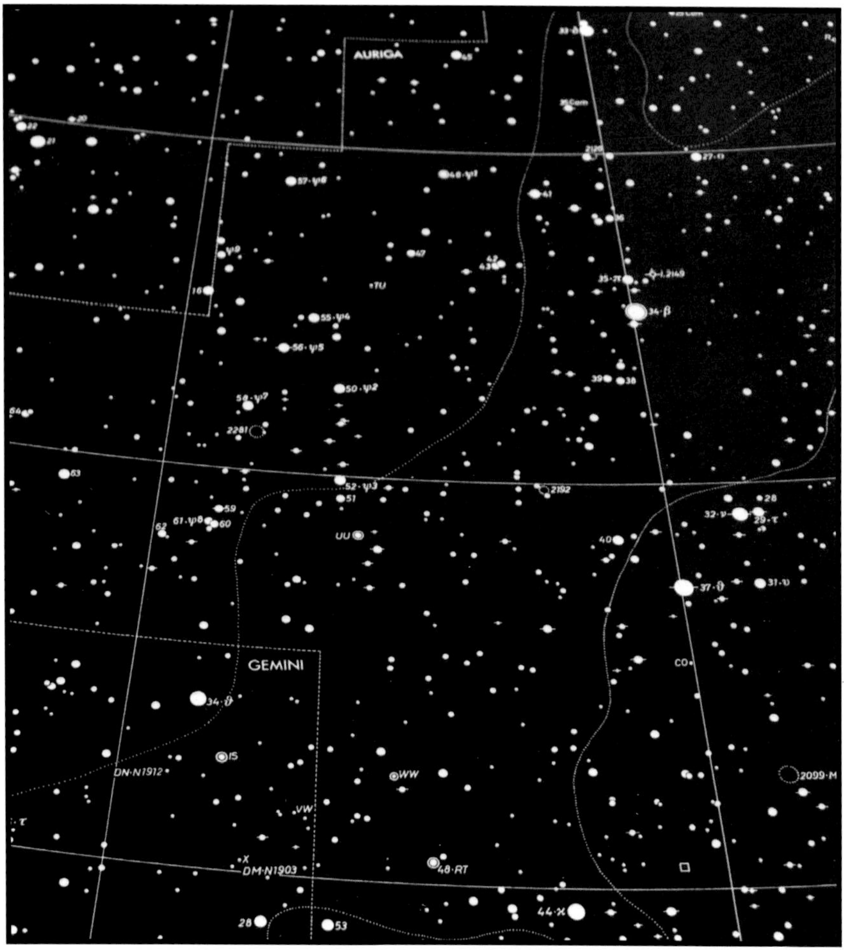

Astronomers study stars.
They use a map to find stars
in the sky.

Some groups of stars are
called constellations.
Constellations form pictures
if you connect the stars.
The Big Dipper is over these trees.

The Big Dipper is a constellation.
Here is what it looks like.

My dad and I look at
the stars at night.
We use a telescope.

Stars look big
through a telescope.
This is what we see.

Stars die after billions of years.
Some stars explode
when they die.
This is called a supernova.

Words to Know

constellation

sky

stars

sun

supernova

telescope